PRIME

POEMS

MYRNA W. MERRON

LYSTRA BOOKS
& Literary Services

ISBN 978-0-9996931-6-2 paperback edition

Library of Congress Control Number 2018962728

"A Letter to Walt Whitman," "Fretting About Frets," "A Bite of the Apple," "A Writer's Block," "A Grave Matter," "Arm and the Man," and "My Neighbor's Garden" have previously appeared in *VOICES*, the literary journal published yearly by Carolina Meadows.

Cover photograph by Meyer Reinish
Back cover photograph by Jacqueline Quay
Book design by Kelly Prelipp Lojk

LYSTRA BOOKS
& Literary Services

Published by Lystra Books & Literary Services, LLC
391 Lystra Estates Drive
Chapel Hill, NC 27517
lystrabooks@gmail.com

For Marjorie Hudson
with appreciation for her guidance,
encouragement, and friendship.

And to all those who have provided inspiration
by their wondrous presence in my life.

CONTENTS

TRAJECTORY

... you are an *I*

— *"In the Waiting Room"*
   Elizabeth Bishop

Prologue

Formal study of math is long behind me, but I recently became engrossed by an article about an obscure mathematician, Yitang Zhang, who solved an intriguing problem regarding prime numbers. This man had pondered for years a question about twin primes, pairs of prime numbers that differ by two. During his quest for a solution, Dr. Zhang did not have a formal teaching job; rather he took bits and pieces of employment here and there—as an accountant or delivery worker—to keep himself afloat. His life's dedication was to solving the problem. Dr. Zhang's work is now considered so significant that he was named a MacArthur genius.

His all-consuming involvement led to me research prime numbers. I knew the definition, having heard it mentioned, probably in grades 4 or 5: a prime number is one evenly divisible only by itself and 1. I never thought of them again. Once I began reading, I understood Dr. Zhang's fascination. Moreover, the word *prime* took on a life of its own. Excellence, of first importance, quintessential, time of greatest vigor in a person's life are just a few of the multiple definitions. And so this little book was born.

Not every poem mentions the word *prime*, or its offspring, or has a prime number embedded. But they all represent significance in my life—joy, grief, introspection. Although I write about my experiences as a woman—it should go without saying, but I will say it—I hope that all readers are prompted to remember his or her own life's prime experiences.

DEFINITION

Questions of Prime

PRIME THOUGHTS I

Who Decides?

Let us now praise prime numbers...
O prime improbable numbers
Long may formula-hunters
Steam in abstraction, waste to skeleton patience
Stay non-conformist, nuisance
                              – Helen Spalding

As time goes by does prime go by?
A weighty question to ponder.
To confront the answer here I must,
not some year way out yonder.

Best by date, sell by date, use by date,
so many milestones to remember,
but are some of these dates purely arbitrary—
who decides if April, May, or November?

Now as a woman of a certain age and more—
far past the phase of prime beef—
(though the best is aged, I believe)
my thoughts turn to primes mathematical
to forestall any intimation of grief.

PRIME THOUGHTS II

My Song

As Whitman sang a song of himself—
himself as a symbol of all people—
I sing a song of myself as prime number
myself as a symbol of all women
divisible by none but me and myself.

Like primes we are building blocks of others—
    numerous in our early years
    thinning out in our middle ages
    becoming rare as time goes by—
    but always remaining prime—
mysterious, nonconforming, without pattern.

I'd like to believe our destiny, my answer:
as time goes by so too a progression of primes
containing all that went before—combining,
including, enriching, and thus enriched by all our times.

Stopping for a Turtle

I stopped for a turtle the other day,
its orange and yellow tattoos
glistening as it journeyed
across a busy road.
Was it oblivious to danger, to humans
encased in shiny armor
careening along the same asphalt?

Or did it just not care,
centered only on its own trek
to get from one side to the other
for food, drink, a warm place to rest, nest?

I wondered whether to step out,
pick it up, and place the creature where
I thought it wanted to go, but instead I accelerated,
skirted around, trusting other drivers to notice,
patiently allow the traveler to find its own way.

The turtle was taking a chance, and so was I.
Living mostly within my warm shell
I occasionally poke my head out to peer
at where I'm going, heedless of danger
or an encounter with an unforeseeable barrier.

Along my path at years 13,17, 29, 37
a few people with fixed intentions
sought to collect me, set me down
where they believed I belonged,
unmindful I needed to find my own way.

Bucket

My

image   flashes

for an   instant

in the   mirror.
Just as swiftly my grandmother's image peers
back at me, not with a long sleep shirt trapped
in her shorts like me, but wearing a shabby old
housedress she hitched up between her legs
thus wondrously transmuting her skirt into
puffy pantaloons, when sore knees pressed
to kitchen floor, stiff brush in hand, sudsy
bucket by her side she scrubbed away
all traces of family footprints with
focus, intensity, and soul great artists
devote to their masterworks

A Letter to Walt Whitman

Dear Walt,

How delightful to meet up with you again. To jog your memory, we first met when I was 16, a very lonely, unhappy 16, reluctantly transplanted to Philadelphia as my family fled a financial doomsday. The gloom lightened when I was introduced to you by an English teacher who demanded memorization and recitation of poetry. So you could say our acquaintance was forced, yours and mine, a sort of arranged marriage. But sometimes these arrangements are felicitous—I fell in love with you. Not right away, not at first sight, only after a lengthy engagement where I learned about you line by line. At first, I thought you a rather narcissistic fellow, tall, good-looking, all full of "I this" and "I that," so self-absorbed as to compose a lengthy poem with "Myself" in the title. Slowly, I began to sway to a rhythm that swept me from one thought to the next, savoring the unrhymed lines—outrageous in the mid-nineteenth century. Your energy jumped off the pages. You appealed to my teen-age disengagement, disenchantment, and my dreams of a gentle world.

Fast forward decades—I was hardly aware of you during those years, so entrapped was I in the "I" that was "me," with poetry easier to read, even tried my hand at composing my own. One day, there you were again, *Leaves of Grass*, a copy from my high school days, had curiously elbowed its way to the front of a bookshelf. I became engulfed by your Civil War poems, harsh, heartbreaking, journalistic, brimming with anguish. Suddenly your "I" transformed into the meaning I grasp you intended—

universal, all-encompassing, empathetic, rousing. At your per-il you dedicated yourself to the wounded in hospitals, young men you dreamed would be the future builders of these United States, now maimed, suffering. (Yes, I know the rumors and truths about you and young men, but that is all irrelevant. Your compassion you gave to these soldiers, no reward desired.)

As I read "When Lilacs Last in the Dooryard Bloom'd" I felt a quickened pulse, combustion, and the embers of my once-love burst into flame, the kind only maturity acknowledges.

Yours,
Myrna

A Grave Matter

Lacking I am in knowledge of physics
but the study of gravity enthralls me,
for life it seems is a constant push-pull
as we strive to maintain our dignity.

Newton watching the fall of an apple
understood attraction of two masses,
what he failed to explain in his universal law
is how this applies to my chassis.

The matter is weighty, grave you might say,
as I observe my frame's aging top
slowly, warily approach my bottom—
despite best efforts, it just won't stop.

Galileo showed that gravity
speeds objects at the same rate;
as I gaze in the mirror I wonder
if chin and bosom will share the same fate.

Now Isaac—I've come to know him quite well—
said for every action there is a reaction,
so though gravity's pull-down is inexorable,
can fate shift with the up-force of traction?

To test my theory I'll go to the gym,
find a bar far overhead,
reach up, stretch and pull and hang—
to challenge gravity I fear and dread.

Though knowledge of physics I surely lack
words of Dylan Thomas I'll certainly heed—
I'll rage, rage against gravity's pull
and maybe, just maybe, succeed.

Vanity

I'd like to be Mrs. Jack Spratt
and gorge myself on sweets and fat,
at 83 it sure would be fun—
but I know it won't, it won't be done.

Lovely singers, actors I have seen
who in their youth looked like string beans,
at 60 shed Spanx, let appetites loose,
now bring to my mind two-legged moose.

Are they more content within, I wonder,
now that applause has ceased to thunder,
to indulge a muffin, slice of deep cherry pie—
while I look, turn away, breathe a very deep sigh.

For although I'm in my ninth decade,
old imagery of myself just will not fade,
so I exercise, eat lean, from fat refrain
because, I confess, I'm wrinkled but vain.

Fretting about Frets
at prime 79

Verb: *be constantly or visibly worried or anxious.*
Noun: *one of a series of ridges fixed across the fingerboard of a*
   stringed musical instrument (as a guitar).

The English language is hard to learn
my evidence is quite simple:
words abound with multiple meanings—
fret is a fretful example.

No one insists I play the guitar,
it's my wish to learn a new skill.
'Tho they say music hath charms to soothe—
 my efforts I fear never will.

Meditation daily bestows peace of mind
'til I pick up that six-stringed guitar,
as my fingers reach for the music's notes,
I note that my talent's sub-par.

My first fret begins when I try for an F
and the stubborn string won't compress—
Too close to the fret, my teacher advises,
Yes, I mumble in childish distress.

When I stretch for G a few inches away
the ping perches harsh on my ear—
Gee whiz is a more apt description I feel
as I strain to suppress a large tear.

Each day I pick up the guiltless guitar
full of optimism and new hope,
but as minutes go by and frets defy me
I fret and I stamp and I mope.

Although the word *fret* sports two definitions
I'm not fooled by this dictionary tale,
for I know *fret* and *fret* are clearly synonymous
each time I attempt a new scale.

A Writer's Block

My fingers are so ready
but where are the letters,
the right words put in right
order to compose a poem?

I feel encased in a block of ice.

So I turn to the experts for advice—
Hilary Mantel says leave your desk,
make a pie, exercise, but don't go to a party
where words of others will pour in.

I cancel my party plans.

Gladwell says to lower expectations.
Angelou pens "the cat sat on a mat"
until her muse offers something better.
In the same vein Gertrude Stein declared
    "to write is to write is to write…"

I start to spout my "blocked" excuses
when I think of electricians who repair fuses,
and plumbers who bill for each minute
 to solve an array of puzzling blocks—

they cannot await the appearance of muses.

So ready my fingers and so am I.
I do ten pushups, bake a blueberry pie,
I lower the bar from excellent to good
write many times *I could, I would, I should,*
and sure enough, ice begins to melt, words begin to fly—

Now I am water—Stein was right.

Sonnet Dedicated to Billy Collins
a prime American poet

A gasp, a sigh, and then relief
when I discovered that even a poet
of honors, prizes, a laureate's wreath
would wrestle a sonnet—but now I know it.

Yet Billy Collins, so like me,
counted down each line, fourteen in all,
but unlike me, he declined with glee
the need to rhyme, and rigid rhythm's call.

Keats penned sonnets from a different stance—
described his true love's ripening breast,
wrote of pain, death, nature—poet's passion—
where desires surge, plunge, reach vales and crests.

Ah then there's Frost with his wit and metaphor,
oh I wish—like him—I could make a sonnet soar.

Edward Hopper and I

I do not believe in the occult.

I repeat this to myself as I stare at the book
of poems that arrives this morning,
this morning that dawns the day after,
the day after I return home from a weekend trip
to the Big Apple, home to many museums,
museums I love and now I can add the Whitney
with its special exhibit of Edward Hopper sketches,
sketches and paintings with their austere lines,

austere lines that echo in the book's staccato poems
about Hopper paintings with their visions of aloneness,
visions of aloneness I contemplated, alone, just the day before
the day before in Manhattan at the Whitney,
the Whitney that had called to me, or was it
Hopper reaching out from The Beyond,
causing me to run forty teeming Manhattan blocks
weighing my need against a plane's rigid schedule.

I don't believe in The Beyond as I do not believe in the occult,
nor does my son when I relay my story. His response,
my son's response to my thank you for the book of poems,
of poems about Hopper's art that arrived the day after,
after my return from New York, is an attempt at reason,
    logic—
to explain why this book of poems, one of an eclectic series
he had gifted me, many months ago for my birthday,
arrives one day after, one day after I viewed
the Edward Hopper exhibit at the Whitney.

I don't believe in the occult, yet Hopper spoke to me.

Breakaway

When you hold on to anything destined to change, you sow the seeds of suffering.
  — Richard Shankman, *The Art and Skill of Buddhist Meditation*

When is the time to stop?
to admit the charade
to cease the game
to slash the chains
that bind to the past
and smother the present

chains formed of links
forged of habit
holding fast to a foundation
eroded by waxing and waning
of the moon, setting of the sun
and tears of despair.

THE SURROUND

Ode to Genius Bar

On a picturesque spring day,
the kind that poets praise,
the kind we wish for after a bitter winter,
I hastened to our local Apple Store,
grim faced, concerned as if a dear friend
had died and I was in need of consolation.

After a lingering illness my laptop screen
had shuddered, became pale, turned white.
I frantically pushed buttons, plugged
and unplugged, consulted with phone techs,
but my efforts yielded no resuscitation, no cure.

I was advised to seek a specialist's care.

At the appointed hour I told my tale
of woe to an intense yet smiling young man
who stood behind the "genius" bar,
a tall counter separating laymen from doctors.
He listened and set about to put my friend
on life support, attaching cables,
applying supple fingers to dormant keys.

I attended carefully to my genius,
trusted his expertise, weighed possibilities.
Despite my white hair and jargon deficiency
he maintained an air of patience, respect.

All about me swarmed a hundred or more
fellow mourners of every age, gender, shade.
We spoke a common language of commiseration,
all Apple users in this together trying to find
solutions to the host of maladies
afflicting our computers, iPhones, iPads—
not merely objects but extensions of ourselves.

On that luminous Saturday we all ignored
sunshine, the glow of daffodils and waving tulips
until, our problems solved, or on their way—
although, alas, some obituaries were written—
we each emerged restored, to find sky blue
without a blemish, the kind of day poets praise.

Arm and the Man

The arm tosses its missile from the car window
with a major league pitcher's finesse.
Rolled neatly inside its plastic wrapper
the newspaper lands with a smooth thud,
never misses its driveway strike zone.

When the driver emerges from the vehicle one day,
rings the doorbell holding an errant paper,
I see a lavish display of long, curly black hair
sitting atop a head of massive proportion,
black and white striped beard of Santa length
almost disguising the features in between

but not quite for I can see the pleasant eyes
the nose, straight, child-like, almost too dainty
for the hirsute visage that looms over
a barrel chest—the chest of a pitcher?—
then my eyes travel to an incongruously tiny waist
and the beginning of a pair of tired trousers
held up by suspenders that strain over the torso.

I thank him for his personal delivery—
he replies with a mumble, a nod.

Each December, holiday time, he writes a letter
of thanks to his customers, a not-too disguised
request for financial appreciation of his services—
a letter so literate in expression and form
it leads me to spin a web about a disinherited
scion, perhaps with an English Lit degree,
who wishes to live simply with common folk
or maybe an author gathering material for a novel
or perhaps he has a Cyrano friend who
ghost writes the letter—am I spinning out of control?—
or is he like most of us, the protagonist of a novel
never to be written, subject of a biography
no historian will ever research, creator of yearly
letters, read once, discarded without a second thought—
an ordinary guy who earns his bread
using his left arm to toss newspapers
to people like me who listen for that daily thud.

Falafel

Pop's Pizza neon beckons my daughter and me.
Inside, wedges of crust with cheese and toppings
keep company with an array of Middle Eastern dishes—
I order falafel.

The serving delivered to our plastic-topped table
on a china dish—four deep brown crusty balls
embellished with fresh greens, containers of vinaigrette,
and pale cucumber yogurt dip.

My first taste brings memories of strolling through
Jerusalem, vendors enticing passers-by with falafel
on wooden skewers—aroma of cumin, coriander
more persuasive than hawkers' cries.

A man with deep olive skin, grizzled beard, a knitted cap
slides into the adjoining table, leans toward me and asks
Do you like the falafel?
Yes, very much, it's wonderful.
My recipe, he smiles.

Without invitation he lingers, chats, tells us
he emigrated from Jordan as a student in the '80s, then
points to the *I Voted* sticker on his shirt, confirming his
pride of citizenship.

We talk about Jordan, Middle East turmoil. He needs
to explain Islam as peaceful, he prays five times a day.
What is your ethnicity?
Polish, I hedge.
Jewish, from my forthright daughter.

Conversation continues unabated.

He despairs the actions of Islamic terrorists as we, to put
him at ease but also truthful, counter with examples
of fanatic followers of other religions, many nations.
Salaam. Shalom.

He plans next month to open his own Middle Eastern restaurant
not a far drive from my home. *Good luck*, I say.
Smiling widely, he carefully packs up my remaining falafel,
adds a container of yogurt dip.

Is falafel a recipe for peace?

Rebellion: On a Cruise Ship I

His eyes glitter
mouth smiles widely
hands push coffee cart
voice calls, "Have some paradise."

Diners chuckle
their delight abounds
he refills again, again
dispersing good cheer.

His shining brown skin
reflects his exertion.
Does playfulness
mask bright intelligence?

Money is thrust,
his fingers reach, clutch,
he calculates slyly,
then his smile freezes.

Now he grasps his worth
servant and funny man,
a temporary diversion,
a few coins for his routine.

I've known him only a week
yet I fear I know him—
his smile disguises rebellion
brewing along with coffee
anger rising with steam
as he pours into cups
held by hands of plenty.

Idle Chatter: On A Cruise Ship II

Conversation not meant for me.
I don't want to listen, not really,
but the words hold a fascination
almost as if I am stealing them,
aware their ephemeral nature
cannot convict me of thievery.

I feel a well of cynicism begin to bubble—
idle chitchat, I almost whisper aloud,
sounds uttered just to obscure silence.

Still, I am captivated.

With my back to the speakers I glean
they are two couples trying to connect
as they dredge up old travel stories
embellish them with little
tales of adventure probably grown
taller with each retelling.

So alien to me is need for idle conversation—
is it not time squandered when
at the end of this week-long sea journey
they will likely never chat again?
That is the way of cruises, I know.

Peals of laughter interrupt my musings,
as if reproach to my silent question.
With a jolt I appreciate their reach for joy
                even for moments,
                        even with strangers.

Always One Step Ahead

You're always one step ahead
I cry out to my grandson
as he tells of reading *The Aeneid*
years ago in the original Latin
while I trudge along, now, in English

But that is the way it should be
I exclaim, explain to the 29-year-old
currently immersed in *The Odyssey*.
I refrain from asking if he is
reading in the original Greek.

This is not the way it used to be.
When he was 8 or 12 or 14
we talked about books, movies,
school issues, life's options—
our conversations gliding smoothly
along pathways where my trove
of knowledge surpassed his.

But the way it used to be
is not the way it is today.
Thoughts I once shared freely
I now ponder before speaking,
feeling diminished by his greater intellect,
as he refers to Proust's madeleines and
research papers on algebraic topology.

This reversal has altered our connection,
his forward steps creating a separation.
The Greeks and Romans educate me
about the constancy of war, infamy, terrible loss.
They also teach me about relationships, now.

Can anyone explain the pain of youth pulling away?

A Letter to Donnette

Dear Donnette,

They say you never forget your first. El primo or la prima. Number 1. I have to agree. I have not forgotten you, my first guardian ad litem case in Florida. To the overworked social worker, you were papers in a file folder entrusted to me: I saw a pretty blond girl of ten, thin, with a blank face. You were not about to let me in, to see what hid behind those blue eyes. I was a guardian but you were guarded. Your decade before we met was filled with troubles I had never encountered—a mother with alcohol and drug problems, your father unknown. You entered the world with impaired DNA and little care followed: no formal schooling, no permanent home. Your two attachments were snatched away—a brother who died under mysterious circumstances and a half-sister taken by her grandmother who didn't want you.

I tried to fathom your depths, found out you liked animals, walks in the woods. At adoption picnics where children seeking parents were paraded before couples seeking children, you were popular; you knew how to sell yourself. But I suffered silently when others tried to teach you what typical 10, 11, 12-year-olds should know socially, academically—and you failed to meet expectations. Expectations based on your golden hair, your lovely face. Despite intensive tutoring, reading was slow, math a mystery. Inside did not match outside. Two prospective adoptions aborted because of selfish desires.

I warned them, pleaded with them, the eager prospective parents, to love you as you were. But they could not help but build castles that you were unable to dwell in. The third couple persevered, showered you with gifts, dressed you as a princess, enhanced your hair with highlights, even changed your name to mark their ownership: you became Nikki—but, as it turned out, not really. After a year, when "Nikki" remained "Donnette," the "parents" settled on another little girl—not quite as pretty but with age-appropriate skills and a stable temperament—and then delivered you back to authorities. The ultimate rejection.

However, I could not let go even after you were finally settled with foster parents who had enfolded you when you were ten, knew your quirks, your limitations, wanted you badly, but could not afford to adopt. Painstakingly, patiently, they taught you the importance of brushing your teeth, bathing, using deodorant, greeting people. They enrolled you in a program that stressed basic work skills. I stalked for a while, in a quiet way, seeking information where I could find it, then moved away and lost contact.

You are now about 32 by my reckoning, the same age as my grandson whose life has been filled with love and nurturance and accomplishment. I hope you have established roots somewhere with people who care about you. I hope that you are able to care for yourself. Sometimes I grieve because I never told you that you are prime. I hope there is someone out there who has.

Always your guardian in my heart,
Myrna

A Letter to Ponce de Leon

Dear Ponce de Leon,

History now says it is myth that you were searching for the Fountain of Youth; because you were so vain you will never escape the story. If there is a whisper of veracity to the tale, you were simply one in a long line of explorers and conquerors seeking to push back the clock, stop the clock, burnish your reputation. If you were truly seeking miraculous waters—not lusting to conquer and plunder indigenous folk, impress royalty, make a fortune—you need not have traveled so far—from Spain to Florida. I know because I have discovered the secret of youthfulness—simply, it resides in the young.

And here is the surprise: it can gush forth while also enhancing its source. I sailed the seas far from home with a teen-aged granddaughter, and discovered the energy, enthusiasm, and elasticity that resided in her were easily transmittable to me, if only I would open my eyes and my heart. Coasting on her font of ebullient can-do attitude, I hiked two mountains, stopped complaining about my aching back, slept more deeply, ate with expansive taste. I didn't ponder, I acted.

Our relationship bloomed, grandmother and granddaughter. Time didn't stop for me, I stopped fretting about limitations of time. Was it the sea air? Could I have made the same discovery at home? I believe it to be true as I report no pain sitting two hours on a backless bench while engaged in heart-to-heart conversation with granddaughter.

Yes, science would say I need more evidence but, Ponce, if only you had set aside your avaricious ambition and made a friend of a nephew or a young sailor, perhaps you would have revealed to the world the secret of Youth transferred, the greatest of discoveries. There would have been no need for gushing waters. You would have been adored not mocked. The myth would have been truth.

Most sincerely,
Myrna Merron

A Phone Call

When a friend calls,
bypasses her usual emails,
I clench when she says,
I have news.

Good news? I ask
startled by her voice.
No. Bad news,
her tone confidential.

I clutch the phone as if
to strangle the message,
deny it life,
set the earth back in orbit.

Her words enter my ear,
travel to my brain, briefly,
plummet to my heart,
seize my guts, where they sit

until my mind functions
again, tries a positive spin
on *surgical exploration,*
knew something's wrong.

Our friendship is an infant, yet
our connection runs deep.
Friends of both head and heart
we share veins of curiosity, humor.

Murmurs of denial would degrade
our rapport. Unbidden, my tongue
spews four-letter words—

what more indicates support?

Wheels

A patina of dust swathes his bicycle,
tired spirit leaning against the garage wall,
tires deflated, empty wicker basket fraying,
pedals stiff at 6 and 12 o'clock.

At 79, its rider buzzed back roads, city roads, highways,
mocking the vision of recumbent retirement
as he eagerly roamed miles to carry out missions—
stamps for this neighbor, groceries for that one.

At 89, his frail frame, curved and lean and spare,
relies on a driver, four wheels and gasoline.
His tired body leans against the handles of a walker
when doggedly he shuffles a few steps to a destination.

He is mostly silent as his resting steed
though he listens keenly when gentle questions
are deflected, answered by his sheltering wife—
his tongue is slow but his eyes report he is no fool.

Now and again the pluck of those bicycling days
tunnels out of his wrinkled brow, hurtles
past stop signs when friends wheel around
to talk about that time when well-oiled pedals
circled and circled around the clock.

In Memoriam

They seem to occur relentlessly
these days as my years surge
and relatives, friends around me fall:
those gatherings that bear witness
to lives no longer lived.

In auditoriums, church halls, living rooms,
the spouses, partners, children, those left behind,
(sometimes the dead themselves in videos)
try to keep alive, for a while longer,
the essence of a person who mattered—
or should have mattered more.

Tears scatter through some tributes,
rolling down cheeks or contained with gulps.
Words, separated by commas, semi-colons—
breathing room to prompt nods, smiles, even chuckles—
elicit comments about the cleverness
of the speaker, even applause. Applause!

Or the freewheeling recitals, desire for one last connection
perhaps to right a wrong, relate a feeling unexpressed,
demonstrate a talent for poetry or guitar strumming,
reveal a secret unknown to other mourners.
(Yes, Grandpa said I was his favorite.)

And what of the dead? Are they present?
Do loving tributes echo, rebound to the spirit?
If so, does the spirit know of bitterness hidden
behind benign facades? Of buried secrets spilled?
Of anecdotes with undercurrents of embarrassment?

Home and silent reflection seem best for me.

A Gift

A new friendship in old age,
a gift that comes without history
when history is filled to the brim
and catching up takes too much time.
It is friendship in the present
a Zen Buddhist relationship
awake to the wonderment
of blooming roses, golden daffodils,
the migration of monarch butterflies
while savoring colors unexpected.

TRAJECTORY

First Love

Just as the snake lover hypnotist began to notice me, sort of, my parents announced a move. My father's business, thriving once, had to be sold.

I was in the middle of my junior year of high school inching, inching toward the precipice of understanding who I was, and now I would have to start over. I didn't know a heart could break into so many pieces and still mysteriously go on beating—I'd be leaving behind my first love.

Some first loves blossom into lifelong relationships, true fairy tales about high school sweethearts still together after thirty, forty, fifty years. These lovers hold hands through life; obituaries list children, grandchildren, nieces, nephews—all testaments to caring and endurance and sometimes, I've discovered on the way to growing up, inertia.

His name was Myles (or was it Miles?) a year ahead of me in high school, slender, dark-eyed, dark hair, olive skin—ascetic (although that word was not in my vocabulary at the time). I think the darkness was what attracted me—I was going through a very gloomy 15-year-old period, reading the Russians, lamenting the fate of Anna Karenina. I wallowed in the aura of desolation, of lost loves.

Weeping for characters thwarted by destiny made me feel more mature, deeper, more soulful than my classmates who cared mostly for parties, football games, cute boys and/or girls. Myles was not cute, although his hair fell over his forehead in a most beguiling way. He was beyond cute.

He was known throughout our high school for his ability as a hypnotist, a skill he liked to demonstrate. Without thinking too long or hard, I volunteered to be a subject, to be hypnotized. (Or did he approach me after noting my adoring, though surreptitious—I thought—glances?) Was it happenstance or fate? Who could know in advance I was susceptible to suggestion? Of course I was, I would have done anything for this object of my affection. And so I became a subject, most times, *the subject*, of his demonstrations for groups of students.

Truly, I believe he did hypnotize me. I didn't fake it—although I admit now I almost certainly would have. During our relationship—strictly platonic despite my yearning—I learned that he was fascinated by snakes. So I became fascinated by snakes, spending hours, days, at the local natural history museum. I even learned to touch them, not to shudder at the sight or be afraid—a set of skills I have made little use of in my life.

If Myles had a glimmer of his irresistibility, he ignored it, focused solely on cerebral issues. He taught me about hypnotism, snakes of course, and recommended I read L. Ron Hubbard's *Dianetics*—I was comforted by the belief that he must have thought I was deep, too. Or he was doing his best to keep a good subject. I grasped at the idea that at least he acknowledged my intelligence—if not, though, the rest of me.

Maybe he would have, given time, lots of time. During Christmas holiday vacation 1950, my family, with little fanfare, relocated hundreds of miles away to Philadelphia. It was a retreat not publicized. I never said goodbye to Myles and I doubt he had any regret. For him, it probably meant recruiting another willing maiden.

My first love, unrequited, not forgotten—the stuff of poems and country music.

FIRST LOVE

First loves deserve a poem
a stanza or two is surely owed them
12 or 20 may have been your age
when heart thumped, face flushed, hormones raged
    Like
       Never
          Before
A stanza or two is certainly due them
if not a sonnet then a different type poem
one that conveys with words and flourishes
the kinds of thoughts that youthfulness nourishes
    Music
       Moonlight
          Kisses
My first love can best be celebrated—
although that word is a tad overstated—
in a five-line verse that may tempt a grin,
the young may read it, there's no mention of sin,
    First
       Love
          Limerick

    There once was a young hypnotist
    who placed me on his subject list
    in a short time I fell
    'neath his dark-eyed spell
    alas never by him to be kissed.

Destinations
December 1950

As the car pulls away the girl looks back
one last time at the white shingle house
appearing so much smaller than the home
that once embraced them. Under the bay window
petunias and portulacas that in summer bloomed,
now December withered.

Resolute, she faces forward, gazes
at her father's broad shoulders bowed
inside the brown jacket. He grips the wheel
as if the road were taking him to salvation,
as if his passengers might leap if he does not keep
a steady course.

Beside him, her mother tight-lipped
in worn cloth coat, stolid as she too looks ahead
afraid a backward gaze would betray a tremble.
She dares not believe this road coursing away from hell
leads to heaven, but perhaps a new beginning, a place
of cleansing.

The girl wedged between two younger sisters
drops her eyes to a book, but this usual escape path
meanders, betrays, cannot pause the tears
from welling, nor block fear family misfortune
would haunt again before she could find her own
flight path.

The girl thinks how lucky her sisters are, cocooned:
the toddler blissfully unaware, trusting, another outing
with her parents; middle sister, self-absorbed,
consults her mirror from time to time, concerned
that the confines of the car, the family, will taint
her beauty.

Silence, heavy silence: no passing remarks about
the scenery, no license plate games, no stories, no songs,
no geography lessons—just five silent people traveling
the same road together toward different destinies with
no bay window or petunias and portulacas.

Sweets Dreams
circa 1969

Crowded in the back seat of our tightly packed
Beetle, my three children eagerly counted
their saved coins and exchanged sweet dreams
of dipping into gigantic glass jars that lined
the rough wooden shelves of their favorite store
in Wellfleet, a glorious way to begin summer—
their pennies would fill brown paper bags
with Gummi bears, sweet tarts, jawbreakers.

As their father guided the car around the familiar bend
of Main Street, yearlong anticipation vaporized
when six lively eyes met smoldering timbers.
A vacation in ruins.

Farewell Tour
Wellfleet, Cape Cod 2015

Like a graying rock star
as age creeps then trots
each year I declare it the last
yet joyous memories of summers past
form a magnetic pole that pulls me to Wellfleet.

My last tour I believe, so I will say goodbye:
To Gull Pond that taught my children to swim
To the dunes that amaze me with their serenity
To the beach plums and rose hips and their nascent jams
To the ocean that brought peace as I strode its shore

To the market with its overpriced tourist food
To the scallops, oysters, and clams fresh from their beds
To the gulls and the crabs, the rocks and seaweed
To the stringent odor of marshes and Uncle Tim's bridge
To Marconi's Atlantic transmission site—hello King Edward VII

To the bike path where the miles display nature's variety
To the many cottages where I have laid my head
To the fragrance of the real Bookstore, and the Bookstore
    Restaurant
To the coffee, raspberry, and maple walnut ice cream by the
    marina
To the blow-up toys, boogie boards, beach towels waving
    hello and goodbye on Route 6

To the actors who overflow the Harbor Theater with talent
To the art galleries and the paintings I can no longer afford
To the thrift shop incongruous amidst designer boutiques
To the family-owned jam and jelly shed standing roadside
    since the '30s
To the sunrise at the ocean and the sunset by the bay

To all of these I bid goodbye,
adieu, auf wiedersehen, sayonara and more
but memories cannot be dismissed with words
and I know in my heart there will never be
a farewell tour.

The Yellow Jacket

Some thirty years ago my mother and I went shopping
with no goal in mind, just time to spend together—
two widows, she inhabiting the status for a year,
I still stunned I was Mrs. without Mr.

Shopping was not a common pastime for us
and had not yet become a national hobby,
so we wandered the new mall aimlessly
chatting and pointing and not spending.

With thoughts of perhaps finding a bargain
we entered a discount store, examined racks
of skirts and blouses with little enthusiasm—
when bright as the sun at a summer mid-day

the yellow jacket winked at me—
a summer hue promising mid-winter warmth
with fleece lining, high collar, deep pockets—
I knew I had found a perfect purchase.

And as the fates would have it, hanging a few
garments away, the same jacket, my mother's size,
in deep orange reminiscent of autumn—
we would be twins when the temperature dropped.

When my mother died more than a decade ago
that deep orange jacket draped a hanger in her
nursing home closet; still, too, my yellow duplicate
kept its space in my closet, memento of a shared day.

This winter the yellow jacket failed to keep me warm
after thirty years of wearing, washing, my bones
grown old and thin. I piled on layers underneath,
but nothing helped. I had to decide its fate.

Back and forth between mind and heart
flew the image of closet barren of that golden hue.
Finally I folded it, placed it in a plastic storage bin
where among other treasures aglow with memories
it awaits its destiny on judgment day.

Matzo Balls

No light as feather matzo balls
float in my chicken soup—
this year there is no chicken soup.

Aromatic slices of brisket do not lay
side by side on a platter awaiting gravy—
this year there is no brisket.

Haroseth, horseradish, parsley, salt water,
hardboiled egg, lamb shank all forsaken—
this year there is no seder plate.

Sweet wine remains unsipped,
Elijah's china cup goes unfilled—
this year the door remains closed to Messiah.

The pile of stained haggadas, long-ago compliments
of Maxwell House Coffee, recline forlorn, unopened—
this year there are no readers.

A box of matzo stares from the pantry shelf
paying lonely homage to freedom—
perhaps next year, with hope, although not in Jerusalem.

Family diaspora, children, grandchildren dispersed.
Change sometimes accepted, sometimes heartbreaking—
only time will tell if *this* change is light as a feather.

Light as a Feather Matzo Balls

4 tablespoons canola oil
4 eggs
1 cup matzo meal
2 teaspoons salt
4 tablespoons seltzer water
2 teaspoons chopped fresh parsley
pinch of pepper

Mix all ingredients together in a bowl. Cover and place in re-frigerator for one hour. Using moist hands, form mixture into balls—you can use a scoop such as an ice cream soup for uni-form balls; I don't like to make them too large.

Bring three quarts of water to a boil and drop the matzo balls into the water, cover and cook for 30–40 minutes. Do not lift the lid while cooking.

Last Night

Last night I dreamed I was awakened
by a baby's moans, found her
wrapped in a light blanket
head to toe
almost like a mummy but flailing
unable to loosen her bonds.

I unwrapped her
careful to hold her tender head
gazed into her calm baby eyes
placed her on her side—
to cover or not to cover?
the dream provided no answer.

There were those nights, many years ago
when my children were young, and I,
inexperienced and unsure and afraid,
would tip-toe to a crib or a little bed,
bend to check on breath so delicate
I could not always hear, and I would curve more,

hold my own breath to create a hollow stillness,
gaze at little chests to determine rise and fall
and then I could breathe again, reassured
that eager little bodies would come tumbling
awake when the sun barely rose in the morning.

So many years later these fears surface
capture my sleep-drugged, hazy thoughts
make me confront again that submerged time
when my first-born child struggled to loose the binds
of cancer, lost her breath, and I could not, did not, save her.

Guardian Angel
for Willie

Forget the common vision
of guardian angels—
ethereal, golden-tressed beauties
trailing diaphanous white chiffon.
(Forget, too, Cary Grant in suit and tie watching
over the bishop's wife, or the twinkle-eyed
bell-tinkler who saved hapless James Stewart.)

My guardian angel wore a cotton dress
many times washed and darned
she would exchange each day
for a starched white uniform,
her prerequisite to beginning
the household tasks I wished done,
no matter the dust or grime.

Dark brown skin, ample body,
cheerful voice, full smile,
she worked without hurry,
took time to eat the lunch I prepared.
Still all was completed by day's end
when once more she slipped
into her shabby travel wear.

To my neighbors she was another
day-worker, cleaning, ironing,
baby-sitting for toddler and infant,
but within my life—I knew, I knew—
she materialized from somewhere
(surely not West Philadelphia)
to save me, to save my family.

Unlike picture book or movie angels,
she received pay for her special powers,
her wages a gift from my father
to ease my despair, exhaustion
of confronting the leukemia daily
unstitching the fabric of my daughter's life,
unraveling the fibers of our family.

I never climbed upon her broad lap
and rocked with her as my children did,
never laid my head on her chest
and disclosed my fears and sorrows;
yet her presence brought comfort,
yet her dignity inspired courage,
and strength to go on, go on.

Her dignity derived from hard beginnings:
black in Savannah, hired houseworker at age 4,
marriage at 14 to older, unloved man.
Hard beginnings that can make or break,
she chose to fashion a life of small blessings.

There is no exact moment when
crisis subsided and we began
to unfasten, she and I. My sick child died.
Then geography intervened to push
us apart. We drifted for a few years
although always she would board the train
in answer to my pleas for help, when my heart
would fray and I needed mending.

I did not know—how could I?—
that the last time I would see her
she would be a guest at the wedding
of my daughter. I was too busy, too busy
to ask about the fabric of *her* life.
Our goodbyes embraced no finality.
She glowed in a blue satin dress.

Until I Die
in memory of Leslie Diane Merron

She will not die until I breathe my last
remembrance of her child's wise gaze
forever in my core's depth gripped fast.

Father, grandparents, and others who cast
a web of love, rest now in graveyard's maze,
but she will not die until I breathe my last.

Younger siblings, in those years long past,
bear no memory of her plucky ways
forever in my core's depth gripped fast.

Her photo on a loved rocking horse casts
a little smile at me that lights my days
thus she will not die until I breathe my last.

The truth I find when wandering the past:
A broken heart is not a fleeting phase,
pain forever in my core's depth gripped fast.

When twilight melds into darkest night
I hear her gasped departing cry—mommy—
forever in my core's depth gripped fast
so she will not die until I breathe my last.

My Neighbor's Garden

Last year I found myself
coveting my neighbor's profusion
of scarlet roses that startled
my eye, tweaked my heart,
so I planted four bushes this spring:
pink, just to be different.

I fertilized faithfully
watered, murmured encouragement,
as spring merged into summer
without hint of a bud
while my neighbor's blooms
taunted me once more.

And I waited and watched
and I wailed as one disappeared
murdered by hungry voles
in the dead of night
and still no roses emerged until
summer, entering its last phase,
prodded one pink bud, then more
from the three survivors,
and now they thrive:
new growth rises from their tips,
hope for next spring's profusion,
a snub to lethal voles.

Life holds curious symmetry, weighting—
four children were planted in my womb.
I nurtured, soothed, encouraged,
then wailed as one disappeared
overpowered by rapacious white cells
in the dead of night
despite my care, my murmurings,
my pleas to all beings holy, and not.

Yet so fortunate am I
to have three survivors
who give pleasure each day
as I bear witness to their growth,
their budding, new blooms
filling my eyes and heart.

CPSIA information can be obtained
at www.ICGtesting.com
Printed in the USA
FFHW011133171218
49890483-54489FF